In The Meantime

A collection of poems

The Hippocrene Society
An Imprint of Neverland Publishing
2014

Printed in the United States of America

ISBN 13:
978-0-9903148-0-6

www.neverlandpublishing.com

In The Meantime

A collection of poems

By

Rowena Carenen

For Elisabeth "Bunny" Heisler who always told the best stories and who was so strong and loved me so well that she made me believe I could be anything.

And for Penelope "Penny" Niven who taught me to seek and tell my own truth. Even, especially, when it hurts.

Table of Contents

I

II

III

Acknowledgements

I

Things that will not make me rich

I don't know when
inane knowledge set up camp
in my cranium, but it has.

I know how Harrison Ford
got his scar (tripped shaving,
bonked his chin on the cabinet)
and the rate of repair
for most cars from 2000-2005.

I don't know pi's decimal places,
but I memorized a recipe
for one that's chocolate mint.

I know how many calories
are in fat-free Cool Whip
(10 per tablespoon)
and the best route to avoid
Atlanta rush hour traffic
(straight on, detours congest).

I don't know the distance
from Earth to Mars,
but the character who appeared
in the most consecutive episodes
of *Star Trek* was a Klingon.

I know that cleaning cookies
out of my computer makes it faster
and to swipe my security card
up fast (down slow bars my entrance).

I don't know how lasik
fixes vision permanently
but I do know how to wiggle
my bottom eyelashes.

I know the addresses and
phone numbers for every house
or apartment I've ever lived; but

I don't know how to talk
to my sister who lived there, too.

Florence, I bleed

Wednesday morning sunshine
peeps through angel wing curtains
and I stretch and wiggle my toes
under new sheets in an old hotel.

Silver ballet flats instead
of pointed-toe practical heels,
a messy bun and my camera
and I'm out with a quick espresso.

Santa Maria Nouvella
and double dark
gelato for breakfast.

I follow the arteries
until they become veins
connecting piazzas and palaces.

I do not pay to see the royals
apartments. The gardens
spread wide in precisely
perfect parameters. No weeds
or wildflowers.
Up and up I hike,
sweat droplets staining
ancient steps, my calves burning
in operatic objection.

Seven hours and twelve miles
bring a Nutella crepe,
two bubble baths,
three local beers,
and four blood stains
in my silver ballet flats.

Grey Spring

Thursday afternoon and the office
tension is thick with lay-off
rumors and cut hours.

White and green coffee mugs,
supposed to make us forget
we now pay for the percolating
morning high, sit on my desk—
discarded attempts at slight-of-hand.

My husband is tired of cleaning
cat litter out of the carpet
instead of heading into some job
that pays better than directly deposited
unemployment.

M*A*S*H reruns get old,
new recipes are expensive and
after a while Oblivion is uninspired.

I slip out from behind my glaring
Dell monitor and sneak some time
in the boss's office to stare out
onto the man-made lake, wishing
the sun was on my back instead
of fading the upholstery of my car.

I count 16 goslings, 5 ducklings
and smile.

Joy Ride

I am tired and want soup
despite the 90+ degrees at 6:30.

I worked too much today, should've
left with the boss but that project
won't complete itself, I say.

NPR oozes soft modern classics
from the speakers in my car. I think
I hear an oboe.

The rust red pick-up
passes me on the way
to Publix on Old Buncombe Road.

We're stopped at the same light, Rusty
and me, his passing doing no good, when
I see the head of a mutt poke out
the back window of the extended cab.

Rusty shifts and turns left and the mutt
bites the air that rushes his face.

Spring into Summer
a reaction to skip foxes "sic transit"

Grass clippings sing
with azaleas and manure,
children hang by skinned knees
on jungle-gyms.
Mornings smell like raspberry smoothies
and sweat drops blossom
on a sidewalk during my run.
Sunsets mean roasted corn
and cold beer on the porch swing.
Sundress straps slip
from my freckled shoulder and the breeze
lifts my blue skirt above my knees,
teasing me away from
finals and papers.
Forgetting winter's death song
and a MasterCard Christmas,
I dance barefoot in the grass.
The Moon and Venus
admire my toenail polish,
sandy pink with silver sparkles.

Secure what?

Karl gave me the heebie-jeebies
since orientation. His lack of
respect for personal space breathed
hot down my neck as I ordered
an egg-white omelet with spinach and
one slice of cheese. He'd shift his girth
and comment on how he needed to "eat
healthy" and I'd wonder "healthy what?"

Sometimes on his rounds he'd
come by my office "just to see."
"See what?" went the thought bubble in my head.

"Two workouts today, huh?" when he'd
check my bags on my way home. I'd fight
down the urge to sling my sweat socks
and make a run for the door. "I should
do that, too," he'd grin.
"Do what?" I was afraid to ask.

Karl was arrested last week.

He was a security guard here
and then he wasn't.

"Wasn't what?"

War Wounds

My breasts bleed pink grins
into my once white sports bra
and green wicking tee. They look
like smilie faces the Joker
would draw on patients
if he were a plastic surgeon.

The Russian Blue licks salt
crystals off of prickly calves, tickling
shins and the backs of knees.

A blister on the ball
of my right foot reopens
in the shower. I cut away white
leathered skin and flush out custard
puss with water and peroxide.

Tomorrow is the day of rest
before I go to battle, again.

Driving with my sister

I held on to the bottom
of the wheel to look cool
like she did whenever Mom
made her take me to Sarah's,
wanting to show I had control
and knew how to navigate
the 1988 Ford Taurus station wagon.

"Let the wheel slide
through your hands at the straight
of a turn."

"NO! Don't let go! Just
let it slide."

I almost threw up.

In 14 years, I've never driven
my sister again.

Time is Not on My Side

Monday night I was disturbed
to discover my worry line
runs straight between my eyes
to the bridge of my nose and
stays put when I'm not worried.

Growing old gracefully
has always been the logical
path, and one I believed
I would meander with ease
sniffing the thyme blooming
in the cracks. I'd never
pluck gray hairs or wear turtlenecks
out of shame. And wrinkles were
to be celebrated as little joys
marking a well lived life.

I bought wrinkle cream on Tuesday.

Are Babies Contagious?

Everyone is pregnant
and thinks I should be.

No one asked me,
or my uterus,
if we were ready
to house a tenant
who made a mess
of the rental property.

It was assumed
that one year of wedded
bliss was enough
and now we must be parents.

My womb and I
have other plans –
wine with dinner,
uninterrupted bubble baths,
a marathon in December.

Engineer Enlightenment

Thermal Sam led
the charge against
redundancy –
the best prove themselves
through ideas and innovation,
not menial tasks and busy
work:

Challenge the old regime,
spiral bound notebooks belabored
with to-do lists –
take quiz, fill out form,
clean screen, and wash windows
so some higher-
up can say "Well done,
you've met our lowest standards."

Do more than check the box
of duties accomplished;
check the box of understanding.

Sam slumps,
expelled all gas
from his turbine.

Sweat-stains without Heroes

Seams repeat, bringing
no new view as miles are logged
on the treadmill's digital counter (3.5, 4.01),
flashing red heartbeats and calories
as I pound rhythm again,
the black steel bar blocking
my escape. Humidity
lines my lungs and I can't
breath condensation, while
I pant, thick drops of sweat
drip off my nose,
splashing the seam.
Not enough support
to keep me from bouncing,
slapping myself in pursuit
of five pounds gone and a size-eight dress.
There it goes again,
that damned seam, reminding me
there is no shining armor sunset,
that my horizon outside the glass wall
of my own aquarium
is an artificial lake with no fish.

For Staci Two Days After Terrorism

We spun,
silly girls,
school girls,
swingin' secretly
behind an abandoned building
on the Wake Forest lawn.
We'd given up
our studies,
her med school applications
lay in a compost pile
and my revisions bled red
next to our book bags.
We lay aside the government's
search for Bukie's brother
in the rubble of Ground Zero.
She pushed us
round and round
on a spinning see-saw
for two.
Staci kicked off
her Birkenstocks
and tucked disgruntled dreads
back beneath a bandana.
I tossed my hair
free from its bun
and laughed as stars swam,
my clogs flung
across the ground

grass staining
my white and blue flowered socks.
We forgot,
for awhile,
that worlds
were collapsing
and chose
to be children
one last night.

Lace Bras Rub Me the Wrong Way

Supportive goes south
when the lace stretches out
the black rose pattern.
The buff background
made of tulle
and sandpaper chafes,
leaving red rivers
around my ribcage.
Delicate straps cut deep
into my shoulders;
the ribbon says girl
and the wire says woman.
Sex sold me satin and lace,
but comfort sold me cotton.

Dear Loan Officer,

If I promise not to run off to the closest
roulette wheel, will you sign off on a minimal
sum? Like a hundred thou?
I won't buy twin albino orangutans
or even customize the Porsche. I'll tithe
to whatever church's pew you ride
on Sunday morning. I'll buy two orphans
Godiva chocolates and take your
in-laws out to Barnhills.
Just write the check, I'll pay
it all back when I sell the movie rights
to "Not-So-Goodfellas," a great novel
I'm thinking about maybe writing
someday. Think of it
as an investment in the next Ben Affleck,
a donation to the arts, Grey Poupon for a starving
student.

Pens and Pints

I want to be the poet
    drinking black coffee in a corner cafe
    huddled over a tattered notebook
    fluctuating from fervent scribbles
    and vacant stares.

Or, maybe I could be the writer
    spouting witticisms in an uptown bar
    slurring a bit over a dirty martini
    or a vodka and cranberry
    wearing Dolce, dropping names.

Perhaps the artist
    swallowing mouthfuls of lager in a Welsh pub
    leaning on a bar stool
    reciting Thomas and wishing for a new canvas
    to pen a rhyme or lyric.

Instead, I take dictation from a lawyer
    in an office that looks like a house
    and is always cold
    because my clothes bunch and hang
    and I can't afford to replace them.

The wrong chocolate cake is worse than no chocolate cake at all

It's not a difficult concept,
dewy moistness
fudgy icing
springy center.

A dry cake
scratches the throat.

Never cross chocolate
with some lesser icing flavor.

If the center does not stick to the fork
send it back.

Satisfaction leaves no crumbs.

Sunday afternoon with Mom

Sermon stomped toes slip
into fuzzy purple socks,
free from pointed heels
and pantyhose.

Yoga pants and a thumb-holed sweater
dis fashion in favor of comfort.

Fresh made chai latte—
sweet soy milk
and orange extract.

The tattered paperbacked story
of a brave mouse and a cowardly
dragon waits on the stained
telephone stand that serves
as a bedside table.

The grey boy finds the crook
of my knee under the old
blue blanket. His contented
grin flashes the peak of his canines
as I scratch the valley of his shoulder blades.

The brown girl blinks
her cream lined eyes,
nesting near my feet, resting
her chin on my heel. Her Janis Joplin
purrs barely scratch out
before drool dampens my sock.

So Long Sister

Third grade I had chicken pox,
pink Popple, oatmeal baths,
TV tray and paint-by-numbers
of white kittens with green balls of yarn
while Mama watched *700 Club*,
prayed for missionaries
(China, Russia, Japan),
cried with the commercial,
begged for 15 cents a day
to feed a kid
swarmed by flies
in the corners of their eyes and lips
bathing in dirty water.
Mama said ok,
Daddy researched:
organizations, CEOs, fund distribution,
and I wrote letters
in cursive
about Jesus healing the lepers,
wishing and praying
for a far off sibling.
But Daddy found corruption
in spokeswoman's false tears
and money-making nonprofits.
There went my Somalian sister.

Ode to the Guy Who Totaled My Car

What were you doing
outside my house
at two fifteen
on a Friday morning
when you woke me
with the sonic boom
of your car colliding
into mine?

How did you miss
Brody's black Mustang
across the street
under a dark Magnolia
but managed to plow
into my great white Oldsmobile
parked under a streetlight?

You, who were too drunk
to know you hit Olga,
sped off on rims
and headed to Petal,
only stopped as the sparks
from your missing tires
caught the cops eye.

So, thank you
for the three and a half thousand
dollars' worth of damage
and the opportunity
to dance deeper in debt
when I buy a used Saturn or Kia.

Sad Satin

I danced for seven years, always
the most dramatic Dying Swan.
And then I stopped, it stopped.

Later, I packed up –
pointe shoes peeked
out of faded pink ballet bag
stuffed with tulle and ribbon,
teal and fuchsia costumes,
someone else's satin slippers
stared back at me.

It had been too long since encore,
and I couldn't get past step two
in Pachabel's Canon,
couldn't stretch knots out
of my tight calves making them
loose, or nail my splits.

She pirouetted in pointe shoes
on waxed wooden stages,
landed each leap on the tips
of toes bleeding inside pink satin.
I didn't know her.

Confessions from a VH1 Junkie

Kid Rock's slow songs
make tapioca out of my flesh,
lumpy and sweetly waiting
for him to suck.

I should know
better than to swerve
into the far right lane
when the croonings of a white rapper
in a wife beater and burnt out
blonde hair that is longer and lighter
than mine come on air, but
I do.

There's something in the sorrow
of a bad boy in love with the beauty queen.
She's high class with pearls
in her belly button,
and he rides his Harley without
a helmet. She left him cold
in August for a badder boy
with more tattoos.

I'll never buy the C.D.,
or even the single,
but I will always turn him up.

Cat Could Be Right

I should scrub the tub
free from the wrap-around
ring and defrost pork chops
to grill with fresh veggies. But
just dried sheets
in a cooled room
smelling of rosemary candles
and the rumbling of a purring cat
put me under in the middle
of a September afternoon.

Foolish Ponies

You could never trust Daddy,
even on regular days Mom
was the gold standard of truth.

But April first, we knew better.
Tuesday morning oatmeal and juice
breakfast before Caitlin caught
the Chesterfield Elementary bus.

"There are ponies in the backyard!"
he called from the kitchen.

Nobody believed him.

Mom took her tea-stained mug,
handle held by super glue,
to the sink.

"Really girls! There are ponies out back."

Caitlin shuffled spoon to mouth,
digging out the purpled goodness
of heat plumped raisins.

But I believed.

By the swing set, I fed
white and dappled ponies
green apples from my hand.

Sundress Instead of Suit

I will buy a peeling plantation
in the land of Spanish Moss,
sweet with the smell
of honeysuckle
wafting into my straw hat.
I will go barefoot
with my red toe nails
bright against the clay.
I will be sunburned, always,
across my shoulders.
The bridge of my nose,
seasoned with freckles,
will be peeling again.
Glasses of sweet-tea replace
Cosmopolitans; an afternoon hammock
becomes my desk.

Ten years to the day

before I married
Nana died.

I wore her
pearls and no veil
with a dress that whispered1940s.

She would've loved
my husband – the way he
tried to teach Drew
that cool guys are smart,
his prayers for my pain,
and the earnest listening
to Granddad's stories.

Granddad missed
his flight and my wedding.

This is not my grandfather.

My grandfather went barrel to barrel
with a Nazi soldier;
tricked all of the grandkids
into drinking his brown water;
wooed women with Rock Hudson looks
and made them sit in the back seat on dates
so his dog could sit up front.

My grandfather took me on narrow boats
down canals through the old country,
bragging to the Brits the age of my college.
He requested "Tiger Rag" from the pub band
because Nana would sing it to her daughter.

Mom feeds her father
coffee in yogurt
because he can't drink
the real stuff anymore.

Stern instructions to swallow
following coughing fits punctuate
breakfast conversations.

Together, she and Dad
change the old man's diapers
every night for three weeks.
They are strangers, but
he thanks them. Most nights.

I offer to help, but they spare
me the vision of the naked Colonel,
afraid it will break my already tortured heart.

Granddaddy scratches out
"safe trip" when I bend
to kiss his paper cheek.

Families and Pharisees

I pace a perfect
square in this cell
of promises and obligations

I made

no noise when the bars
built the perimeter
of space allowed me

by my self

I find no solace
because the demands
begin again

I lose

my place in this structure
a self-imposed vice
twisted by myself
and others

fail to adhere
to their rules my rules
of perfection

I scream silently
until my desire
to please presses
out a final breath

Possession

Words raced about the wrinkles
on his face and in her head
and fought for their place
on the page.

Poems must be written
and stories need be told.

Rest was not an option.

Frantic scribblings
on cigarette paper
memorized and burned.

Truth-telling is a responsibility.

Menopause Ain't So Bad

I've done it twice now,
beating my mother
to the hormonal ride.
I should write a book,
a tip guide for older women.

I was only 20 the last time.

The night sweats soak sheets,
but light cotton pajamas
paired with a fleece blanket
at the foot of the bed
warms my toes when the chills come.

Morning sickness
and my doctor prescribed
daily naps. I craved chocolate,
carrots and Mylanta.

One more ticket for the Estrogen train
and then I'm done.

Taps

I made it through the scripture
fine, and "How Great Thou Art"
only blurred my vision.

My spike heels made divots
in the grass of the memorial garden
and Devin held my elbow
to keep me steady.

But then the flag.

The soldiers held it
as if over an imaginary casket,
folding and creasing.
Mom stepped forward
for the family,
mascara making
rivers on my cheeks.

Shots and taps
and I broke. Silent sobs
shake my shoulders.

One more duty and I'm done
and I can begin to mourn.

For Jeremy

I am two years too late
to mourn you.

We kept an *X-Files* dossier
on you because silly girls
couldn't suss out the giant
who whispered encouragement
but couldn't keep eye contact long
without blushing.

You sought the worth in words
with the subtlety of a spider's
silky stream.

My poems were packed with pepper
while your palette craved
thyme, ginger, and curry.

You showed me a delicate
line delivered in elegant verse
lingered in a listener's ear.

I am two years too late
to thank you.

Hero Pill

It was a gift
from an 87 year old man
two weeks before
the crowd of cronies, admirers
and fame followers
put him to rest
in a mausoleum that presidents
would envy.

Some said he was the savior
of a metropolis, others
believed he was the nemesis
of truth and justice.

At the funeral, behind
the onlookers, slouches a man
who would be handsome
if he didn't hide his face
beneath a gray fedora,
black framed glasses,
and a well-weathered overcoat.
Home movies from 50 years of
train wrecks, plots for global
domination, and near nuclear
destruction play out before him
and he smiles.
He fingers the lead-
lined case in his pocket

wondering what Lois
would've said about the crypt,
the Ecclesiastical verse invoked,
but her ashes were spread across
the Planet years ago.

In Solitude the man pours
a glass of Vitamin D whole
milk, winces as he opens the case
and swallows the sugar-coated
green capsule.

Ninety ain't Nothin'

My grandfather, the giant,
is now 5'6"
with vanishing calves.

Ninety next month
and planning on one hundred plus,
he flirts with the waitress at Friendly's.
He wouldn't take me with him
for pancakes, disappearing
before I got up,
so she would flirt back.

This is his first summer
not long-boating through
the canals of England and Wales
in more than a decade.

Mom and I cleaned his closet
amidst violent and vehement
protest that the yellowed shirt
and see-through shorts
were just fine. A retired
Air Force Colonel swore
like a sailor.

I thought he had forgotten
Caitlin's graduation,
but he had only forgotten
her name.

Twenty-first Tributes

The weekend of my 21st birthday:

Mama held my hand,
braided my hair;

my sister sent pink flowers,
a cross from Prague;

Rhiannon cried,
nearly failed her final;

Daddy prayed,
hair went from black to silver;

doctors scraped my uterus with lasers,
gave me the video.

On the Death of Colonel Henry Blake

Not two episodes earlier, Mrs. Blake sent reels,
their daughter was seven, his blonde baby
growing into her daddy's little girl.
Martinis all around, Hawkeye served.

No notice and Henry gets discharged—
shoulder slaps instead of hugs,
Franks sulks to Hot Lips in the O.R.,
Father McAhey gives the Holy Mother's blessing,
and Henry gets to go home.

As his chopper spins off, the wounded come
and surgeons must re-thread their needles,
stitching shut bullet holes
in a tent with poor lighting.
Radar announces a helicopter crashed,
no survivors.
The good doctor dies, the soldiers
are sucker punched,
and a telegram is sent state-side.

thursday 2 am

chilled metal table
warm leather straps
cuff wrists and ankles
wrench—bloodied joints
circus clown music—
doctor dancing—
knees high
head back
pirouettes on tile

no anesthesia
sweat induced dreadlocks
stick to clammy forehead
limp while
exaggerated scalpel
dices deep
ovaries ripped free
eggs intact
tossed through air—
two points in the biohazard bin

uterus
gone, but
pulses translucent
blue baby
chokes strangles,
swish in red plastic.

Osip

a lifetime before
his arrest
he had his cobbler
stitch razors
in his soles
just in case –
suicide as survival

Mandelstam walked on death for years.

Tidal Screams

Madness takes the room
and delirium whispers in a stranger's ear:
"It comes and goes, the screaming."

The captain suggests holding
hands, taking naps, singing songs;
madness takes the room.

Experience teaches never to presume
a lessening of the fear, incompetence—
"it comes and goes, the screaming."

Elbows in, oars out for rowing,
praying that a break will come.
Madness takes the room.

No answers to questions that loom
in their thought balloons :
"It comes and goes, the screaming."

Against the desks, heads are beating
in captain's rhythm, testimony that
madness takes the room.
"It comes and goes, the screaming."

Sweets and a Stay of Execution

"six weeks more"
dash against the jagged
edges of years of hormone
therapy, slicing surgery
and hours in stirrups
that have no
"giddy-up" to take
me away
or at least the disease
infected organs.
six weeks more.

six weeks more
of experimental pills
and painkillers, parents
crying and boyfriend's
chocolate while
best friend re-books
trips to vienna
for an operation moved
back again
six weeks more.

Clean

I wonder what the soap
was made of that
convinced them to walk
without a fight
into gas showers;

whose idea it was to
create a charade—
work camps that did no work,
digging holes that were filled
the next day,
hospitals that didn't heal
but tested thresholds,
tattoos on the Generals'
favorite girls
delicately and with
great care in the center of the left wrist—
so elaborate that it even
had props.

Fruit Stand

A woman in the market,
pinching apples smelling melons,
was pregnant
and I wasn't
never will be.

My uterus is a clementine
with thumb print scars
bruising the juicy meat
permanently browning the surface
of the skin, peeled by lasers.

My ovaries are figs—
gnarled and bitter
from too much exposure on
trees in the south
of nowhere, slashed
full of holes from
careless shears.

My eggs are passion fruit
turned sour on vines
now lacking in
nourishment and health—
tart and wrinkled,
ruined.

My vagina is a persimmon—
dripping white wounds
failing to stretch
for fertilization or purging
staining hospital sheets and gowns

Namesake Tokens

Daddy's mother died
years before I entered the clan,
but she left me things:

white Woolworth's nametag,
two hand-stitched handkerchiefs:
blue blossoms tipped in summer
green and palest pink-edged cream;
a New Testament with glinting gold
pages and her name inscribed inside.

Once there was an Israeli onyx ring
with rosebud scrollwork kissing
the black stone. But Lori lied and stole it
off the radiator during my birthday.

Oh, but I hope for:

patience to not kick the chair
out from under a silly son
faking his own hanging;

kindness to a neighboring stranger
during a double
shift in the crowded
check-out line barking
commands and whispering epithets;

gentleness to a husband
stained from the mines, contaminated
with cancer and cruelty;

grace when all her teeth
were yanked at twelve because dentures
were cheaper than fillings.

These are things I pray
she left me, this woman
whose name I bear.

III

I sleep face-first

in the pit of his arm,
one hand under the pillows,
one across his scar.
His hands support his head,
our feet hold soles,
and I dream to his breathing.

I dream of nothing.
Pricks of his whiskers
on my neck wake me while
a rough hand grips my thigh.

We've turned in our sleep,
his ribs a xylophone against my spine,
his knees lock in mine.

Next door an alarm goes off,
and my neighbor laces her shoes
for a morning run.

I try to slip out
under the vise of his left arm,
afraid to stir him. But I fail
and decide to stay,
to sleep late instead.

Jupiter's Storm [1]

Jupiter has no rings,
too many moons govern,
he commits to nothing –
gravity's pull is weak and
there is no peace in trajectory;
asteroids pock his surface.

Jupiter pulls
away from Earth – with her
one moon – and she submits
to the pull of another.
Gravity weighs down
her core, hooking her into a dull orbit.

She can't say
how/why she made him mad.

Jupiter spins insane showers
sopping her hair, soaking her clothes.

She can't stand in the fury, brown eyes broken.
Spine hunched, head down, weathering the wind.

Red rage.

---

[1] *Scientists note that a storm on Jupiter is large enough in magnitude that it can completely destroy ten planets the size of Earth.*

A small planet lost
in the violence of an overwhelming orb.
In her green, she lacks
the atmosphere to sustain his ever-
lasting showers.

Jupiter's storm can encompass ten Earths.

For Alexa on Her 29th Birthday

Again. I want to go shopping
for blue leather purses that don't
match anything but are pretty. Again.

Before. You loved khakis and crisp
White shirts with black boots and belts
cinched tight, understated pearls. Before.

Now. You're in love with fancy flats
and townhouses downtown, wooly coats
and ear pieces for your phone. Now.

Later. I will be "Aunt" to your children
who are all smarter than I and know
my voice and face, not a picture. Later.

Still. I tell you my secrets, confess
my sins over pizza and root beer. You
listen and love me. Still.

Defeated by Beauty

I lost the touch
of gristles on the back
of my neck tracing
down my spine to my
top hip
   kissing coffee
of the Times and adding
Barbasol to the shopping
list next to Dove soap
   signing two
names to Christmas cards
and juggling schedules
for drinks with neighbors.

She wasn't prettier, she just didn't know the lies.

Colonel Love

Granddaddy was a dragon:

his snoring scared little girls
nearly wetting the bed
for fear of creeping by
his cave;

his orders law at home,
at the office, on the water –
barked with flame-tinged
adjectives.

But Bunny was a dragon-slayer:

perfect pink lips under blue
and tweed driving caps
for the convertible Firebird
with a trunk big
enough for the wheelchair.

Morning Sustenance

I've never been much
of a breakfast eater, but
when he told me to swing
by Shipley's Doughnuts
on my out of town
I said I'd try.

"Heading home for Christmas?"
he asked, leaning out of the drive
through window, my eyes still
bleary at 5:15 a.m. He laughed
at my grunted affirmation, handing
me a box of seven different doughnuts:
cinnamon and sugar, glazed, chocolate,
chocolate glazed, and cherry filled.
"Orange Juice, for something healthy,"
tossed in with a laugh.

We'd had one, maybe
two conversations that contained
more than class schedules, wilted
weather observations, and cat health,
and he was already feeding me
as I headed North on I-59.

Ode to Orange Juice

It hit me the other day,
like a fit of giggles
from an eighth grade girl,
that we've been friends
longer than we haven't.

I don't know what
that means, if it has to mean
anything at all, but I do know
that the day you laughed at me
when orange juice shot out
of my nose in the Miller Middle
School Cafeteria, we became
friends.

You always tittered at my weird
comments in classes about economy
and *The Price is Right.* Together
we defended Sylvia's sanity
with the righteousness of sophomores
and you never judged me, scolded me
or mocked me for being silly, quiet
or scared.
I should've trusted you more
when you told me to watch
out for viciousness dribbled
in chocolate. Chocolate made
me lazy, as comfort food

is prone to do. And instead
of singing "I told you so's"
you held my hand and took
me to terrible movies

and made me laugh
so hard that Diet Coke
shot out my nose.

Molly's Merriweather One

I already loved you
when your legs, swaddled
tight, kicked in my arms.

Twenty-two hours before,
you were a fairy's heartbeat.

We prayed for you
planned for you, even
partied for you – gifting
your mom with too many socks
and too few burp cloths.

But until your daddy
(and it is important for you
to know that he
is most certainly a daddy
not merely a dad or a father)
handed you to me
and you squirmed and settled
against my pink scarf worn just for you,
I didn't know how much.

Suicide is Painless is my Lullaby

I fall asleep sometime after
the choppers come over
Radar's cap and before
Hawkeye's first quip.

My head rests on your chest
or the pillow cradle
you create for me
in our Swamp.

I never wake
when you slide in
hours or minutes later
and you don't stir,
except for the occasional
sleepy declaration,
when I leave in the early hours
wishing the road signs
were pointing me home.

Sheets and Sweat

Real love is sleeping
in sweat dampened sheets
because I sleep on your
side, smelling your shampoo,
until you slip in beside me.

Every morning we swap
as I sneak out, tucking my
pillow in place, pulling
on shoes and shorts
for a pre-dawn run.

You hold my replacement,
sleepily scooching into
the indentation I left behind.

I am jealous.

Missing Alexa

The count is up to seventeen
emails so far today and she's
only been in the office
for thirty minutes.

There's snow in Chicago
and red leaves with green grass here
but we're both wearing warm
gray sweaters and jeans
with black boots and argyle socks.

She laughed when I told
of cinnamon and clove brine
and white paper-wrapped
turkey innards.

But typed laughter leaves me lonely.

New Love Song

I don't need chocolate
as a declaration of sweet sentiment,
and roses don't define
the bloom of affection.

Instead, fresh cat litter
in the over-used once white pan
whispers unfiltered loveliness
as clean air breathes through the house.

Carpets that were grey yesterday
are made red again and the dishwasher
hums bits of salads out of bowls
and days-old ketchup off plates.

I know what to do if you die—

I'll call my parents, yours followed
by Kevin and James. You'll be buried
at United Methodist in Waynesboro
in the suit I bought for Stephen's wedding.

I'll move to a smaller apartment, windows
in all of the rooms for the cats. Your favorite
shirts will be my pajamas, donating the rest
to Goodwill. I'll light vanilla candles every
night when I get ready for sleep and doze
to *M*A*S*H* reruns.

I'll go back to work and smile when I should
and run a marathon to get away.

But.

I don't know how to breathe
if you aren't.

Little Starr

You have your own song
sung around the world,
tiny voices note the wonder of your existence.

I know not what you are
but I do know you are loved
and lovely.

Your heartbeat was your mother's song,
faster than her trombone,
but that horn brought you into her world
and made your daddy love her.

I love your mom, too, you know,
down here, miles away from ultrasounds
and ducky filled showers of tiny sandwiches,
booties in green and yellow.

Your room will be filled with books:
*Make Way for Ducklings, Goodnight Moon,
Where the Wild Things Are*
and one day I will read you stories
of four children and their adventures
in a wardrobe.

Date Night Redefined

Nightly I unpack-repack
two gym bags
while cats bang their skulls
on my chin and shins
until I stop everything
to justify their self-esteem

You lounge back against
double pillows and shams,
home for hours,
and tell me Jim's an ass
but the new office software
is click-clacking into
a workable system.

I tell you arrogant engineers
storm my office
brandishing their weapons -
time demands and assumptions
of warrant -

You tell me your best
man is getting a divorce
and the un/packing stops
mid-fold.

I curl up, head in the pit
of your arm and listen
and sigh a prayer of thanks-
giving for you, for us,
for our daily date night.

Toothache, a love poem

Fever made his face
the color of old cinnamon
gum and his left cheek
puffed-up, a lumpy bubble.

The dentist prescribed a cocktail
of Vicaden and Valium an hour
before pristine pliers popped
the abscessed tooth from its strong-
hold on his jaw.

I was hilarious, apparently, to him
while I helped him upstairs
and made a nest of our moss
green easy chair. "Apathy" was a riot
and so was the letter "v"
until the drugs delivered
their promise to induce
drowsiness.

He slept like a five-year-old,
intent on healing the hole
left in his head, sweat
puddling in the wrinkles
of his forehead. Our cat,
curled in the crook of his arm,
stayed with him for three hours.

Dinner, a mess of monotony
disguised as soft foods, cushioned
round two of the double v cocktail.

With slurred consonants
he apologized, for what,
I wasn't sure. But I loved him
for the effort.

No Me

I wonder if you would've known me
had I strolled by
on a summer evening
or maybe you would've
sat at my table in the library
as I dove into the lives
of dead poets,
my hair in a bun
my bifocals on the tip of my nose;
or maybe I would've sat
in the back of your father's church
to hear the Word
from the Ragin Cajun.
I was a girl
when last we met
in the crowded room
of someone else's house
for someone else's party.
I am a girl no longer.
I have faced demons
that you'll never know
conquered diseases
beaten back disorders
survived disasters.
I wonder if you could've ever known me?

Hopeful Romantic

first kisses
   awkward nose rubs
   mismatched lips
   teeth clash and clink
last kisses
   cheeks flushed posey
   hungry lips before fast
   taste lingers on buds
late nights
   cinnamon tea talks
   undercover giggles
   spoon sighs
early mornings
   toasted muffins in orange marmalade
   holey flannel robes
   hands held under newspapers

I believe in short hellos and long good-byes.

Molly's Merriweather Two

I dreamt last night of tattoos –
fairy wings done in a delicate blue
on my shoulder blades
in honor of you.

I will read to you of
forests found in wardrobes,
tell stories of fauns
and a pilgrim's progress,
of a mouse's valor
and a dragon's tear.

Oh little one,
we will have glorious
adventures before the Lord's
prayer sweeps you into sleep.

You will be so buoyed
by love, that your heartbreaks
will break mine, too.

Road to a Wedding

She said she'd rather go to the beach
on our way to her "I do's".

I had two swimsuits in the back
and the weather on the gulf
was nice this time of year.

She said maybe we could go
to New Orleans, drink Mimosas,
and eat beignets at Café du Monde.
We could shop in the Quarter,
wear white sundresses and big straw hats.

She said maybe we could go
back to Hattiesburg –
she could sleep on the couch.

I said okay.

But the car took the exit anyway,
I laced up her corset, held her bouquet,
kissed her cheek.

And toasted their happily ever after.

Pastime with Peter

Thursday night class
Dad called
and I wanted it to be him
but of course
it wasn't
and I wasn't surprised.

Instead I'm on the way back
from church
wanting to laugh at his Dippity Doo'ed hair
and James Dean earnestness
at want to kiss other girls
and expecting me to wait.

It's Junior High
the first time he held my hand
as the communion dish,
bronze plate with blood velvet center,
was passed between us.

I didn't even know
his name when he grinned
and winked
during his father's sermon,
telling my sister that I
"was going to be a babe when I grew up"
and I blush my first innocent pink
staring at the Gospel.

Lots of firsts:
"you know you're beautiful, right?'
"when we get married,
we'll open a restaurant
just to do the dishes together."

Hint of Camel Lights in Listerine
burns my tongue
in alcohol and stale smoke
he promised to give up
for me, for basketball,
when we kissed.

An unexpected guest
at someone else's party
slouching in a corner
of the Crosby's sun porch,
glared because I sat with Jack
and laughed with Robby.

Fingertips traced the scar
on my right knee
his head in the hollow
of my belly
as the sky turned tombstone grey
and the storm danced
before us.

My phone sang
and I slide into the backseat
of his silver Buick Sky-
lark and watch the windows fog.

Partners

You drove fast, following Dad
to the hospital while Mom
rode in the ambulance with Granddad.

I rambled on about sweat
showing through my yellow
tee-shirt and forgetting the chocolate
while putting four books in my purse.

Usually, I drive calmly,
speak in smooth tones,
comfort the crazies.

You did it
so I could breath.

A Poem for Kate's Poems

I drank
your words tonight –
an alcoholic running
from Betty Ford:

slurped:
she is a headhunter
and I am her game,
and
this Philadelphia Brownstone loves me like a
mother;

guzzled:
this is not exactly what the self-help books
would call self-mutilation
and
I'm in love and in danger
I can't be okay if you aren't;

as they lapped
along my tongue
a robust red wine
that burns a bit
when gulped

but warms the aching hole
made by your absence
from this arctic dorm
that demands wool sweaters
in a summer
of dull Valdosta days.

I believe in Casablanca

He was January without
twinkling snow
or even a cool breeze.
When asked about my
romantic sensibilities
I responded in clichés:
pink satin, white lace,
overstuffed teddy bears,
vanilla candles,
champagne and strawberries.

Separation is inevitable,
as Rick found out
twice.
And although "beautiful friendships"
take a bit of the bite out,
they don't ease like
a long strong drink
from a bitter and fiery glass.

I had just about begun to believe
in happiness
when my best friend
opened wide for my
boyfriend's release
a month into our ever after.

So I pull up a stool
to Sam's piano,
slur Billy Joel,
throw darts at their
engagement notice,
and become a regular.

Decomposition of Joanna Klink "Untitled"

In the room a wind is easing.
When I imagine where
the light goes as we speak,
I think of the *The Bell Jar* and
Pride and Prejudice and pockets,
closets opening to sand.
The Mocking Birds are still
and overhear us. What
hides itself is somewhere
nesting in the trees of silence,
too strong to be chopped down,
as you turn to touch the breakfast table
or believe me when I say I'm fine.
Words settle in our lungs
and we breath our sorries.

Benadryl and Toilet Paper: A Love Poem

Pretty pink pill put
me to sleep in our foam
covered bed, nestled neck
deep in down comforter
and blue sheets.

2:47 Wednesday morning,
eyes bleary with white crusty
goo, I stagger into the master bath
hunting Kleenex or at least Charmin
to clear my nose of the ick
that has taken residence in my skull.

I inhale cinnamon and musk
and maybe vanilla, from bath balls
put away from Christmas,
as I breath deep, prepping my lungs
for an ear popping blow.

My face leaks lazily, frustrating
me further, I stumble back
to bed, tasting holiday spices
caught in the back of my throat,
reminding me that I am loved,
drippy nose and all.

Cardiogram

Let me unzip your chest
and climb ribs
to nest behind the breast bone.
I'll send you smoke signals
from the tepee of your lungs
and go dancing in the open spaces
where bones and blood stand guard,
bouncers to your heart.
Your heart is my colony
and I am the Magellan of your ventricles.
I'll plant my flag dead center.

Acknowledgements

First, I would like to thank my parents, John and Lisa Carenen, for loving me and supporting me and teaching me to find my own voice and be bold. For being proud of me, even if I didn't go into computer programming.

A heartfelt thank you to my writers group for being willing to read multiple drafts of multiple poems and always striving to give honest and helpful feedback. I may not be Raffian, but I do hope to be one day.

Next, I'd like to thank Melissa Thornley Ryon, photographer and friend extraordinare. Not only did you deliver the most amazing cover, you read every single iteration of this book, even in the throes of chaos and academia. I love you dearly.

Thank you also to Alexa Starr and Christine Faust who have loved and supported me fiercely for many years. You are both warriors and I'm so very glad you are on my side. And whose children inspire more poems than this book could contain.

To the folks of Neverland Publishing, your patience, understanding and support leave me without words but with more gratitude than I have space to share.

And lastly, I want to thank Devin Copeland who taught me so much about love and myself. Without you this collection would never have come to be.

Made in the USA
San Bernardino, CA
10 October 2014